James H. Trumbull

The Defence of Stonington, Connecticut

against a British squadron

James H. Trumbull

The Defence of Stonington, Connecticut
against a British squadron

ISBN/EAN: 9783337313289

Printed in Europe, USA, Canada, Australia, Japan

Cover: Foto ©Andreas Hilbeck / pixelio.de

More available books at **www.hansebooks.com**

THE

𝔇𝔢𝔣𝔢𝔫𝔠𝔢 𝔬𝔣 𝔖𝔱𝔬𝔫𝔦𝔫𝔤𝔱𝔬𝔫

(CONNECTICUT)

AGAINST A BRITISH SQUADRON,

AUGUST 9TH TO 12TH, 1814.

———

"Vixere fortes ante Agamemnona."

HARTFORD:

1864.

CONTENTS.

INTRODUCTORY NOTE.

THE repulfe of a Britifh fquadron, at Ston-ington, by a few undifciplined volunteers, having only two effective guns, imperfectly protected by a low earth-work,—and this repulfe accomplifhed without the lofs of a fingle life,—was not the leaft glorious achievement of the War of 1812-14. The fiftieth anniverfary of the action is clofe at hand. Few who witneffed,—only three or four who participated in it, furvive. In this day of great events, when armies and navies are gathered on a fcale of magnitude of which our fathers never dreamed,—when from the heights of modern fcience, we look back to the guns and the fhips of war of the laft generation, as to the toys of childhood,—when we are in the very crifis of a war greater in itfelf, and waged for a grander iffue, than the world has hitherto witneffed,—it is not furprifing that fo few find leifure or inclination to look from the prefent to the paft, or to recall to memory the heroifm of their fathers.

Yet there are fome for whom the ftory of *The Attack* has not yet loft its intereft. They learned it in childhood, from the lips of thofe who fhared the perils and the glory of the action. They grew up, amid affociations which could hardly fail to kindle an honeft pride in their birth-place. To them, the "Tenth of Auguft" was not merely a fchool-holiday, but an anniverfary entitled to equal honors with Independence Day itfelf. They have helped draw the "old Eighteens," through the ftreets of the Borough, in folemn proceffion to the fite of the demolifhed Battery. They have feen the cherifhed Flag—pierced and torn in a dozen places by the enemy's fhot,—float again from the flag-ftaff, in honor of the day: and fome of them were ftanding by when "Old Hickory" bared his head to falute it, and bade the citizens preferve, with all care, this precious memorial of the courage and patriotifm of their townfmen.

It is for thefe—the companions of my own fchooldays,—and in honor of the volunteers of 1814, that I have reproduced fome of the contemporary accounts of the attack and defence of Stonington. The firft (pp. 9–20) was written by Col. Samuel Green, the publifher of the *Connecticut Gazette*, who vifited the Borough during the action, and obtained his knowledge of facts of which he was not an eye-witnefs, from the actors themfelves and from official fources. This account, printed in the *Gazette*, of Auguft 17th, was copied into many of the newfpapers in the northern ftates, and appeared in Niles's *Weekly Regifter*, November 5th, with fome additional particulars.

Following this, are copies of the mufter-roll of the Borough company of militia; the official account furnifhed for publication by the magiftrates, warden and burgeffes (pp. 24–32); and a letter from Capt. Amos Palmer, chairman of the citizens' committee of defence, to Mr. Crawford, fecretary of war, containing a concife narrative of the action. Philip Freneau's *Battle of Stonington*,— though not of the higheft order of lyric excellence,— challenges favorable comparifon with many of the loyal effufions which have found their way to the public, during the prefent war; and will be welcomed as an old friend by fome who value patriotifm more than poetry.   T.

Hartford, Conn., July 28th, 1864.

THE DEFENCE OF STONINGTON.

[From the Conn. Gazette, Aug. 17th, 1814.]

RECORD OF THE EXTRAORDINARY ATTACK ON STONINGTON.[1]

NEW LONDON, AUGUST 17, 1814.

ON Tuefday the 9th inftant, at 5 P. M. the *Ramilies*, 74, *Pactolus*, 38, a bomb fhip, and the *Difpatch*, 22 gun brig, arrived off Stonington, and a flag was fent on fhore with the following note—

> " On board his Majefty's Ship, Ramilies,
> Stonington, Aug. 9.

TO THE MAGISTRATES OF STONINGTON.

Gentlemen—One hour is allowed you from the receipt of this communication, for the removal of the unoffending inhabitants.

THOMAS M. HARDY.[2]

This notification was received by two magiftrates[3] and Lieutenant Hough of the drafted militia, who went off to meet the flag. The officer was afked whether a flag would not be received on board. He faid no arrangements could be made. They inquired whether Com. Hardy had determined to deftroy the town. He replied that fuch were his orders from the Admiral, and that it would be done moft effeftually.

When the gentlemen reached the fhore, a crowd waited with great anxiety for the news; which being ftated, confternation flew through the town. An exprefs was defpatched to General Cufhing,[4] at New London. A number of volunteers haftened to collect ammunition; others ran to the battery, which confifted of two 18 pounders and a 4 pounder, on field carriages, with a flight breaft work, 4 feet high. The fick and the aged were removed with hafte: the women and children, with loud cries, were feen running in every direftion. Some of the moft valuable articles were haftily got off by hand, others placed in the gardens and lots, or thrown into wells, to fave them from the impending conflagration. The fixty minutes expired, but the dreaded moment did not bring the attack. Nelfon's favorite hero and friend was feized with the compunftions of magnanimity;—he remembered what ancient Britons were; he remembered that fomething was due to the charafter of Sir Thomas M. Hardy. Three hours in faft elapfed, when at 8 in the evening the attack was commenced by a difcharge of fhells from the bomb fhip. Several barges and launches had taken their ftations in different points, from whence they threw Congreve rockets, and carcaffes. This mode of attack was continued inceffantly till midnight ; and the fire was returned occafionally from the battery, as the light of the rockets gave opportunity with any chance of fuccefs.

The few drafted militia which had been fometime ftationed there, under command of Lieutenant Hough, were placed in the beft directions to give an alarm in cafe a landing fhould be attempted. During the night the volunteers and militia had affembled in considera-ble numbers ; and the non-combatant inhabitants had generally removed to the neighboring farm-houfes, in the momentary expectation of feeing their abandoned dwellings in flames. It was a night of inexpreffible anguifh to many a widow and orphan, to many aged and infirm, whofe little pittance they were now appa-rently to lofe forever. But Providence directed other-wife. This compact little village of 100 buildings had been for four hours covered with flames of fire and bomb fhells, and not a fingle building was confumed nor a perfon injured.

At the dawn of day on the 10th, the approach of the enemy was announced by a difcharge of Congreve rockets from feveral barges and a launch, which had taken their ftation, on the eaft fide of the town, and out of reach of the battery. Several volunteers, with fmall arms and the four pounder, haftened acrofs the

point, fuppofing the enemy were attempting a landing.
Colonel Randall of the 13th regiment, who at the time
was moving towards the battery with a detachment of
militia, ordered them to affift the volunteers in draw-
ing over one of the 18 pounders to the extreme end of
the point ; the fire of which in a few minutes compelled
the barges to feek fafety in flight.   During this time
the brig was working up towards the Point, and foon
after funrife came to anchor, fhort of half a mile from
the battery, (or more correctly, the breaftwork).   Our
ammunition being foon exhaufted, the guns were fpiked,
and the men who fought them, being only about 15 or
20,(5) retired, leaving them behind for want of ftrength
to drag them off.

The brig now continued deliberately to pour her 32
pound fhot and grape into the Village, without our
having the power of returning a fhot, for an hour, and
the bomb ketch occafionally threw in fhells.   A frefh
fupply of ammunition being obtained, the 18 pounder
was withdrawn from the breaftwork, the vent drilled,
and the piece taken back again, when fuch an animated
and well directed fire was kept up, that at 3 o'clock
the brig flipped her cable and hauled off, with her
pumps going, having received feveral fhots below her
water line, and confiderable damage in her fpars, &c.
During this action between the eighteen pounder and
the brig, Mr. Frederick Denifon was flightly wounded
in the knee,(6) by a fragment of a rock, and Mr. John
Miner, badly burnt in his face by the premature dif-

charge of the gun. The flag, which was nailed to the maft, was pierced with feven fhot holes,[7] the breaft-work fomewhat injured, and 6 or 8 of the dwelling-houfes in the vicinity effentially injured. At this time a confiderable body of militia had arrived, and Briga-dier-General Ifham[8] had taken the command; the in-habitants had recovered from the confternation of the firft moments; and were deliberately moving off their furniture and goods. At 1 o'clock the Ramilies and Pactolus had taken ftations about two and a half miles from the town, when refiftance appearing hopelefs, the Magiftrates as a laft refort applied to the General for permiffion to fend a flag off, being impreffed with the opinion that there must exift fome latent caufe of a peculiar nature to induce a commander who had here-tofore diftinguifhed himfelf for a fcrupulous regard to the claims of honorable warfare,—to induce him to commit an act fo repugnant to found policy, fo abhor-rent to his nature, fo flagrant an outrage on humanity. The General, we underftand, would not fanction, nor did he abfolutely prohibit, a flag being fent. They, therefore, on their own refponfibility, fent on board the Ramilies, Ifaac Williams and Wm. Lord, Efquires, with the following letter.

Copy.)   *Stonington August* 10, 1814.

To Sir Thomas M. Hardy,

Sir—Agreeable to notice received from you yefter-
day, this town is now cleared of "unoffending inhabitants," and they feeling anxious about the fate of their
village, are defirous to know from you, your deter-
mination refpecting it.   Yours, &c.

Amos Denifon, Burgess.
William Lord, Magistrate.

The deputation proceeded on board the Ramilies,
and fhortly after an officer informed the boatmen that
they might return to the fhore, as the gentlemen would
be landed in a boat from the fhip ; and that Captain
Hardy had declared that no further hoftilities would
be committed againft the town.   After remaining on
board an hour, or more, the deputation were conveyed
in a flag from the fhip, which was met by one from the
fhore.   They brought with them a very fingular and
extraordinary communication.   An exact copy cannot
at prefent be obtained, as official etiquette will not permit ; but having read it when it was received on fhore,
as far as memory ferves us, it was as follows :

On board H. M. Ship Ramilies, off Stonington, Aug. 10.

Gentlemen—You having given affurances that no
torpedoes have been fitted out from Stonington ; and
having engaged to exert your influence to prevent any
from being fitted out or receiving any aid from your

town : If you fend on board this fhip tomorrow at eight o'clock, Mrs. Stewart, wife of James Stewart efq. late His Majefty's Consul at New London, and their children, I engage that no further hoftilities fhall be committed againft Stonington ; otherwife I fhall proceed to deftroy it effectually.—For which purpofe I poffefs ample means.

T. M. HARDY, Capt.

This letter was received indignantly. No anfwer was given.   It was a fact well known that no torpedoes have been fitted out at Stonington, and that the inhabitants are unfriendly to the fyftem ; but neither individuals nor the town have power to prevent their reforting to that place.   The condition *fine qua non*, is truly *tragi-farcical.* Neither the town of Stonington or the State of Connecticut, had any legal power to comply with it, which Capt. Hardy well knew.   And if Stonington Point with its rocky foundations had been in danger of being blown up, fcarcely a voice would have been raifed to have faved it on fuch difgraceful terms. The firft duty of a citizen we are taught in Connecticut, is to obey the laws.   Mrs. Stewart is under the protection of the government of the United States, and the petition of her hufband for a permiffion for a departure is in the hands of a proper authority, who will undoubtedly decide correctly in the case.[9]

Our countrymen at a diftance, from the importance Capt. Hardy has attached to the circumftance of Mrs.

Stewart's being fent off to the Britifh fquadron, may poffibly apprehend that fhe has received infult, or fignified fome fears for the perfonal fafety of herfelf and children.—So far from this being the fact, no lady ever experienced greater civilities from the citizens ; as no one has better deferved them. And her feelings during the proceedings at Stonington, demanded the fympathy of her friends.

By the terms offered by Capt. Hardy, it was impoffible to difcover whether he was moft doubtful of his ability to accomplifh the destruction of the town, or defirous of a pretext to fave it. He affured the gentlemen who accompanied the flag that this was the moft unpleafant expedition he had undertaken.

The truce on the part of the enemy having expired at 8 o'clock on Thurfday morning, a flag was foon after obferved at the battery to be coming on fhore, and there not being fufficient time to give information of the fact at head quarters and receive inftructions, it was determined by the officer then commanding to fend a boat off to receive the communication. Mr. Faxon, of Stonington, took charge of the boat, met the flag, and offered to convey the difpatch agreeable to its directions. The Britifh officer, Lieut. Claxton, queftioned his authority to receive it ; enquired whether Mrs. Stewart would be fent off; and faid he would go on fhore. Mr. Faxon replied, that he knew nothing of Mrs. Stewart ; and that if he attempted to proceed for the fhore, he would undoubtedly be fired on. He continued his courfe, when a centinel was directed to fire forward of the boat, but the ball paffed through the after fail. They immediately put about and fteered for the fhip; the lieutenant fwearing revenge, for what he termed an infult to his flag.

An explanation of the circumftance was immediately tranfmitted by General Ifham to Capt. Hardy, which he received as fatisfactory.

At the moment, a flag had ftarted for the Ramilies,[10] from the civil authority of the town, which was received on board; by which was fent the following letter :—

Stonington Boro', Aug. 14, 1814.
To Thomas M. Hardy, *Commander of H. B. M. fhip Ramilies.*

Sir—Since the flag went into New London for Mrs. Stewart, and family, General Cufhing, who commands at New London, has written, we are informed, to the Secretary of War on the fubject, and it is our opinion that the requeft will be complied with. But whatever may be the refult of the communication from Gen. Cufhing, you will be fatisfied it is not in our power to enter into any arrangement with you refpecting her.

From yours, &c.

Isaac Williams,
William Lord, } *Magiftrates.*
Alexander G. Smith,

Joseph Smith, *Warden.*

Geo. Hubbard, } *Burgeffes.*
Amos Denison,

3

To this letter, Capt. Hardy replied verbally, that he should allow till 12 o'clock for Mrs. Stewart to be brought on board.(11) At this time the principal part of three regiments of militia had arrived, and the town was perfectly secure against a landing.

At 3 o'clock, the bomb ship commenced throwing shells into the town; and being out of reach of our cannon, the General withdrew the militia excepting a guard of 50 men who were ordered to patrol the streets for the extinguishment of fire, should any happen. The bombardment continued till evening.

On Friday morning the bomb ship renewed her operations a little before sunrise, while the Ramilies and Pactolus were warping in. At eight o'clock the frigate opened her fire and was soon followed by the Ramilies. At this time the cannon were ordered to be moved to the north end of the town, where they would have been serviceable if an attempt had been made to land under cover of the ships. This was a very hazardous service, as the party would be entirely exposed to the fire of the enemy. Volunteers in sufficient numbers instantly offered their services; among whom were upwards of twenty of the Norwich artillery. The command of the party was entrusted to Lieutenant Lathrop, (12) of that corps. They marched to the battery and brought off the pieces without the smallest accident; exhibiting all the steadiness which characterises veteran soldiers.

This tremendous cannonade and bombardment continued till nearly noon, when it ceased; and about four o'clock the fhips hauled off to their former an-chorage.

During the fucceeding night a large force was kept on guard, in the expectation and hope that a landing would be attempted. The militia during this afflicting fcene difcovered the very beft difpofition, and were eager to take revenge of the enemy or.facrifice their lives in the conteft.

It may be confidered miraculous that during the fe-veral attacks, while fo many were expofed to this ter-rible and protracted bombardment and cannonade, not a perfon was killed, and but five or fix wounded, and thofe but flightly. Among the wounded is Lieutenant Hough[13] of the drafted militia.

On Saturday morning the enemy relinquifhed the hope of burning the town, weighed anchor, and pro-ceeded up Fifher's Ifland found.

The volunteers who fo glorioufly fought in the bat-tery, deferve the thanks of their country. No men could have done better. Their example will have the happieft influence.

About forty buildings are more or lefs injured, 8 or 10 effentially fo; and two or three may be confidered as ruined. The damage was principally done by the brig. Many fhells did not explode, feveral were ex-tinguifhed. The Congreve Rockets which were fright-ful at firft, loft their terrors, and effected little.

The inhabitants, fearing another attack, have not returned to their dwellings, and their defolate fituation calls loudly upon the philanthropy of their fellow citizens.   If a brief fhould be granted for collections in the churches of the State we truft very effential aid will be furnifhed.   Nineteen-twentieths of the inhabitants, it is faid, have no other property than the r dwellings.

A Nantucket man has been on board the Britifh fleet to redeem his boat, and learned that the Difpatch had 2 men killed and 12 wounded; her lofs was undoubtedly much greater.

NAMES OF VOLUNTEERS.

[From the Conn. Gazette, Aug. 24th.]

The following is handed us as a lift of the volunteers (tho' prefumed not entirely perfect,) of thofe who fo bravely ftood the brunt of the attack of Stonington Point :—

Of *Stonington :—*

Capt. George Fellows,	Gurdon Trumbull,
Capt. Wm. Potter,	Alex. G. Smith,
Dr. Wm. Lord,	Amos Denifon jun.,
Lieut. H. G. Lewis,	Stanton Gallup,
Enfign D. Frink,	Eb. Morgan,

John Miner.

Of *Myſtic* :—

Jeſſe Deane,	Jeremiah Holmes,
Deane Gallup,	N. Cleft,
Fred. Haley,	Jedediah Reed.

Of *Groton* :—

Alfred White,	Frank Daniels,
Ebenezer Morgan,	Giles Moran.

Of *New London* :—

Major Simeon Smith,
Capt. Noah Leſter (formerly of the Army),
Major N. Frink,   Lambert Williams.

From *Maſſachuſetts* :—

Capt. Leonard,   and   Mr. Dunham.

[From the Conn. Gazette, Aug. 31ſt.]

By an error of the compoſitor, the following names were omitted in the liſt publiſhed in our laſt paper, of volunteers who ſo greatly contributed to the glorious defence and preſervation of Stonington, viz. :—

Simeon Haley,	Thomas Wilcox,
Jeremiah Haley,	Luke Palmer,
Frederick Deniſon,	George Palmer,
John Miner,	Wm. G. Buſh.
Aſa Lee,	

There were probably others, whom we have not learnt.

[From the original in the Comptroller's office, at Hartford.]

MUSTER ROLL of the 8th Company of Infantry under the command of CAPTAIN WM. POTTER in the Thirtieth Regiment of Con. Militia in ſervice of the United States, at Stonington, commanded by Lieut. Col. WM. RANDALL, from the 9th of Auguſt when laſt muſtered, to the 27th of Auguſt 1814.—

Names and Rank.	Commencement of ſervice.	Expiration of ſervice.	Alterations and Remarks ſince laſt muſter.
Captain, William Potter,	Aug. 9	Aug. 27	
Lieut. Horatio G. Lewis,	" 9	" 27	
Enſign, Daniel Frink,	" 9	" 23	detached for ſervice and ordered to N. London, Aug. 22.
Sergeants :			
Francis Amy,	" 19	" 27	
Charles H. Smith,	" 9	" 27	
Peleg Hancox,	" 22	" 27	
Gurdon Trumbull,	" 9	" 27	
Corporals :			
Azariah Stanton jr.,	" 16	" 27	
Junia Cheeſebrough,	" 9	" 27	
Joſhua Swan jr.,	" 22	" 27	
Privates :			
Phineas Wilcox,	" 9	" 23	detached for ſervice & ordered to New London, Aug. 23.
Hamilton White,	" 9	" 27	
Henry Wilcox,	" 9	" 23	detached for ſervice & ordered to New London, Aug. 23.
Nathan Wilcox,	" 9	" 27	
Samuel Burtch,	" 9	" 27	
Jonathan Palmer,	" 9	" 27	
Andrew P. Stanton,	" 9	" 27	

Name	Enlisted	Discharged	Remarks
James Stanton,	Aug. 9	Aug. 27	
Thomas Breed,	" 9	"	Volunteer exempt, difcharg., Aug. 17.
Amos Loper,	" 9	"	Volunteer exempt, difcharg., Aug. 20.
Samuel Bottum, Jr.,	" 9	" 27	
Benj. Merritt,	" 9	"	Produced certificate of parole on 15th Aug. & difcharged.
Elifha Cheefebrough Jr.,	" 9	" 27	
Chriftopr. Wheeler,	" 9	" 23	detached for fervice & ordered to New London, Aug. 23.
Amos Hancox,	" 9	" 27	
Zebadiah Palmer,	" 15	" 27	
Nathl. Waldron,	" 15	" 27	
Thomas Spencer,	" 19	" 27	
Nathl. M. Pendleton,	" 20	" 27	
Simon Carew,	" 22	" 27	
Elifha Faxon Jun.,	" 22	" 27	
Ebenezer Halpin,	" 22	" 23	detached for fervice & ordered to New London, Aug. 23.
Afa Wilcox Jun.,	" 22	" 23	detached for fervice & ordered to New London, 23 Aug.
Warren Palmer,	" 22	" 27	
Jofeph Bailey Jun. } *Waiters,* 9	"	" 27	Waiter to Capt. Wm. Potter.
Nathl. Lewis, }	"	" 23	Waiter to Lieut. G. Lewis.

I certify, upon honor, that this Mufter Roll exhibits a true ftatement of the 8th Company ; and that the remarks fet oppofite the men's names are accurate and juft.

WILLIAM POTTER, *Capt.*

We certify upon honor, that the foregoing Mufter Roll exhibits a true ftatement of Captain William Potter's Company; and that the remarks fet oppofite the men's names are accurate and juft.

> John Jamieson Jr., *Afft. Adjt. Genl. &*
> *Muftering Officer, per order.*
>
> Wm Lord, *Regimental Surgeon.*

————

Account of the Attack, furnished for publication, by the Magistrates, Warden and Burgesses.[14]

[From the Conn. Gazette, Sept. 7th.]

Stonington Borough, Aug. 29, 1814.

Mr. Green—In relation to the extraordinary attack of the enemy, of the 9th inft., on this village, the public have been furnifhed with various accounts; and though the circumftantial and generally correct account given in your paper [of the 7th of Auguft,] precludes the neceffity of a recapitulation of the whole tranfaction, yet this village having been the object of the attack and refentment of Sir Thomas, the Magiftrates, Warden and Burgeffes refiding therein, feeling deeply interefted that fome official document comprehending a fupply of fome facts not given, and alteration of others, and a general ftatement relative to the whole, fhould be publifhed,—offer the public the following statement :

On Tuefday afternoon of the 9th inft. anchored off our harbor, the frigate *Pactolus*, the *Terror*, a bomb fhip, and the brig *Difpatch* of 20 guns. From the difficulty of the navigation in Fifher's Ifland Sound, we have been generally impreffed that such fhips of war dare not approach us ; but the prefumption of the enemy has created new fears, and we think it our duty to fay, that further means of defence and protection ought to be afforded us ; this we have often requefted. Various were the opinions refpecting the object of the enemy, but foon all was fettled. A flag was difcovered to leave the frigate and row towards the town. The impropriety of fuffering them to come on fhore was fuggefted ; and a boat was immediately obtained, Capt. Amos Palmer, William Lord Efq., and Lieut. Hough of the detachment here, felected, and the flag of the enemy met by ours, when we received the following unexpected and fhort notice—(This not having been furnifhed the public correctly we give it at length :)

His Britannic Majefty's fhip PACTOLUS,
9th of Auguft, 1814, *halfpaft* 5 *o'clock, P. M.*

Not wifhing to deftroy the unoffending inhabitants refiding in the town of Stonington, one hour is given

4

them from the receipt of this, to remove out of the
town.

T. M. HARDY, *Capt. of H. B. M.*

Ship RAMILIES.

*To the Inhabitants of the Town of
   Stonington.*

From the date of this communication it will appear
that Commander Hardy was himfelf on board the Pactolus to direct the attack ; the *Ramilies* then laying at
anchor at the weft end of Fifher's Ifland.   The people
affembled in great numbers to hear what was the word
from the enemy; when the above was read aloud.
The enemy in the barge lay upon their oars a few moments, probably to fee the crowd and if fome confternation might not prevail.   Whatever effect was pro-
duced, this we know, that Sir Thomas's " unoffending inhabitants" did not agree to give up the fhip,
though threatened by a force competent, in a human
view, to deftroy them, when compared with the prefent
means of defence in their power.   It was exclaimed,
from old and young, *We will defend.*   The male citizens, though duly appreciating the humanity of Sir
Thomas, in not wifhing to deftroy them, thought proper to defend their wives and their children, and, in
many inftances, all their property ; and we feel a plea-
fure in faying that a united fpirit of defence prevailed,
and, during the fhort hour granted us, expreffes were
fent to Gen. Cufhing at New London, and to Col.
Randall,[15] whofe regiment refided neareft to the fcene

of danger. The detachment ftationed here under Lieut. Hough was embodied; Capt. Potter, refiding within the Borough, gave orders to affemble all the officers and men under his command that could be immediately collected. They cheerfully and quickly affembled, animated with the true fpirit of patriotifm. The ammunition for our two 18-pounders and 4-pounder was collected at the little breaft-work erected by ourfelves. The citizens of the Borough, affifted by two ftrangers from Maffachufetts, manned the 18-pounders at the breaft-work, and alfo the 4-pounder. One caufe of difcouragement, only, feemed to prevail, which was the deficiency of ammunition for the cannon. This circumftance, however, together with the fuperior force arrayed againft us, did not abate the zeal for refiftance. Such guards of mufketry as were in our power to place, were ftationed at different points on the fhores. In this ftate of preparation we waited the attack of the enemy. About 8 o'clock in the evening they commenced by the fire of a fhell from the bomb-fhip, which was immediately returned by a fhot from our 18-pounder. This attack of the enemy was immediately fucceeded by one from three launches and four barges, furrounding the point, throwing rockets and fhot into the village. This alfo was returned as often as, by the light of the rockets ftreaming from the barges, we could difcover them. Affifted by the above military force, the inhabitants alone, fome feventy years old, defended the town until about 11 o'clock; and had it not been for

the fpirited refiftance manifefted, a landing no doubt,
would have been effected. At this time Col. Randall
had arrived, and having iffued orders to the militia under his command, they began to affemble, and from
the fhort notice given them were truly prompt and active in appearing at the poft of danger : fome volunteers had alfo arrived. From this additional ftrength,
the apprehenfions of the enemy's landing, in a mea-
fure vanifhed. Their fhells, rockets and carcaffes, having been prevented from fpreading the deftruction
intended, they ceafed firing them about 12 o'clock.
All was ftill from this time until day-light. A fire of
rockets and fhot from the launches and barges again
commenced, which was fpiritedly returned from our
artillery taken from the breaft-work, in open view of
the enemy and expofed to their fhot, on the end of the
point, and they [were] compelled to recede. This
truly hazardous fervice was nobly performed. Col.
Randall having been prompt in his appearance, as
were all the officers and foldiers of his regiment, they
were now organized, ready and eager to receive our
invaders. From the fpirit manifefted among the citizens, volunteers and foldiers, and the judicious arrangements made of the troops affembled, had a landing
been attempted a good account would no doubt have
been given of them. We were now alfo affifted by
numbers of volunteers. The barges having receded
from the fire of our four and eighteen-pounder on the
Point, they were taken back to the breaft-work.

About 8 o'clock in the morning of Wednefday, the Brig [*Difpatch*] hauled within half a mile of our breaft-work, and opened a well directed and animated fire. Our few guns being now well manned by citizens and volunteers, from Stonington, New London, Miftick and Groton, they were ready to receive her. Her fire was returned with a fpirit and courage rarely to be equalled,—and of those gallant fouls who ftood this conflict, we can only fay, they glorioufly did their duty. Heroes having fo nobly acted, with ours, will receive the plaudit of their country. What effect fuch bravery had on the enemy, will appear from the fact, that the brig was compelled to cut her cable and retire out of reach of our fhot. Her anchor has fince been taken up, with a number of fathoms of cable. No attack was afterwards made by the brig. This conteft with the brig (called the *Difpatch*), continued on our part from the breaft-work until the ammunition was expended. To this circumftance, unfortunately for the village and mortifying to thofe fo gallantly engaged in the defence, may be attributed the principal injury fuftained by the buildings. For two hours or more, fhe kept up a conftant fire without having it in our power to return a fhot : during which time, we are confident, had there been a fupply of ammunition, fhe would have been taught the ufe and meaning of her name.

The further particulars which tranfpired on Wednefday and Thurfday, having been noticed by you, in the publication above referred to, very correctly, the public muft be fatisfied without any comments from us. In the publication of the tranfactions of Friday, we have difcovered one error. Amidft the combined fire of the Ramilies, frigate and bomb-fhip, Lieut. La-throp and volunteers from the Norwich Artillery, in fact did proceed, to undertake in affifting to get off the cannon from the breaft-work, but they met other brave lads who had accomplifhed this hazardous duty. The praife therefore of this performance, however they may have diftinguifhed themfelves in other duties, is not correctly beftowed.

In paffing the proceedings of Thurfday and Friday, we would not overlook the fingular communication received from Commodore Hardy, which preceded the fire on Thurfday. Two fubjects efteemed very im-portant by Sir Thomas feem connected, Torpedoes and Mrs. Stewart,—a lady we prefume worthy of the notice even of Commodore Hardy. But a demand made on thofe with whom, it was well known, no power exifted to comply, is not a little extraordinary : befides, this communication is totally different from and uncon-nected with the one it was fent as an anfwer to. It would appear from reading the documents, that affu-rances were given that no torpedoes ever did, or ever fhould, go from this place. This was not the fact ; no promifes or confeffions of any kind were ever made. To this fingular letter no general reply was given ; that part, only, [was] noticed, relative to Mrs. Stewart.

The enemy left us on Friday, without having accomplished that destruction which they told us was to be effected. The damage done the buildings is estimated at about four thousand dollars. This would undoubtedly have been much greater, had not the volunteer vigilant firemen[16] from Capt. Potter's company before mentioned, and others, continued firm at their posts, determined that not a flame kindled by those fiery engines of the enemy but should be extinguished,—and it was done. This duty, perhaps, was as important and useful for the salvation of the village, as any performed during the conflict.

The list of individuals given to the public as distinguishing themselves during the contest, we esteem very imperfect. To give a correct list of all those who did distinguish themselves in the various duties that were performed, is not easy to do; we shall therefore forbear. Having thought proper to bestow a just tribute of praise on the officers and soldiers of the 30th Regiment, who first arrived at the scene of action, it becomes us to express, also, the high sense which we entertain of the services and judicious and soldier-like conduct of Brigadier-General Isham, and the officers and soldiers of the 8th and 20th Regiments, assembled under his command.

During this protracted bombardment, nothing more excites our astonishment and gratitude than this, that not a man was killed on our part. We understand from good authority, the enemy had a number killed and feveral badly wounded,[17] in this unprovoked attack upon us.

We have made fome eftimate of the number of fhells and fire carcaffes thrown into the village, and we find there has been about three hundred. The amount of metal fired by the enemy will exceed, we think, fifty tons. About three or four tons of bombs, carcaffes and fhot have been collected.*

WILLIAM LORD, } *Magiftrates.*
ALEX. G. SMITH, }

JOSEPH SMITH,   *Warden.*

AMOS PALMER,   ⎫
AMOS DENISON, ⎪
GEO. HUBBARD, ⎬ *Burgeffes.*
THOMAS ASH,   ⎪
REUBEN CHESEBROUGH, ⎭

* " Some refpectable citizens from motives of curiofity weighed feveral fhells &c., and found their weight to be as follows.

One of the largeft carcaffes, partly full of the combuftible,	216 lb.
One of the fmalleft fort do.	103
One of the largeft kind empty,	189
One of the largeft bomb fhells,	189
One of the fmalleft do.	90
One, marked on it (fire 16 lb)	16

One of the largeft carcaffes partly full, was fet on fire, which burnt half an hour, emitting a horrid ftench ; in a calm the flame would rife ten feet. Some of the rockets were fharp pointed, others not, made of fheet iron very thick, containing at the lower end fome of them a fufee of gre-nade, calculated to burft, and if they were taken hold of before the ex-

LETTER FROM CAPT. AMOS PALMER, TO THE SECRE-
TARY OF WAR.

[From Niles's Weekly Regifter, Oct. 21, 1815.]

DEFENCE OF STONINGTON.

The defence of Stonington by a handful of brave citizens was more like an effufion of feeling, warm from the heart, than a concerted military movement. The refult of it, we all know, and it afforded fincere delight to every patriot. But the particulars we have never feen fo accurately defcribed as in the following concife narrative from the chairman of the committee of defence, to the Secretary of War, of which we have been provided with a copy for publication.—*Nat. Intelligencer.*

"Stonington Borough, Aug. 21, 1815.

To the Hon. Wm. H. Crawford,
Secretary of War.

SIR :

The former Secretary of War put into my hands, as chairman of the committee of defence, the two 18-pounders and all the munitions of war that were here, belonging to the general government, to be ufed for the defence of the town,—and I gave my receipt for the fame.

plofion, might prove dangerous ; one or two perfons received injury in this way. They appear to contain a greater variety of combuftibles than the fire carcaffes.

As there is no military officer here, it becomes my duty to inform you [of] the ufe we have made of it. That on the 9th of Auguft laft [year], the *Ramilies* 74, the *Paɛtolus* 44, the *Terror* bomb-fhip, and the *Defpatch* gun brig, anchored off the harbor. Commodore Hardy fent off a boat, with a flag; we met him with another from the fhore, when the officer of the flag handed me a note from Commodore Hardy, informing that one hour was given the unoffending inhabitants, before the town would be deftroyed.

We returned to the fhore, where all the male inhabitants were collected, when I read the note aloud; they all exclaimed, they would defend the place to the laft extremity, and if it was deftroyed, they would be buried in the ruins.

We repaired to a fmall battery that we had hove up —nailed our colors to the flag ftaff—others lined the fhore with their mufkets.

At about feven in the evening, they put off five barges and a large launch, carrying from 32 to 9 lb. carronades in their bows, and opened their fire from their fhipping, with bombs, carcaffes, rockets, round, grape and cannifter fhot, and fent their boats to land under cover of their fire. We let them come within fmall grape diftance, when we opened our fire upon them, from our two 18-pounders, with round and grape fhot. They foon retreated out of grape diftance, and attempted a landing on the eaft fide of the village; we dragged a fix-pounder that we had mounted over, and met them with grape, and all our mufkets opened fire on them, fo that they were willing to retreat the fecond time. They continued their fire 'till 11 at night.

The next morning at feven o'clock, the brig *Defpatch* anchored within piftol fhot of our battery, and they fent five barges and two large launches to land under cover of their whole fire (being joined by the *Nimrod* 20 gun brig). When the boats approached within grape diftance, we opened our fire on them with round and grape fhot. They retreated and came round the eaft fide of the town. We checked them with our fix pounder and mufkets, 'till we dragged over one of our 18 pounders. We put in it a round fhot and about 40 or 50 lbs. of grape, and placed it in the centre of their boats as they were rowing up in a line and firing on us. We tore one of their barges all in pieces ; fo that two, one on each fide, had to lafh her up, to keep her from finking. They retreated out of grape diftance, and we turned our fire upon the brig, and expended all our cartridges but five, which we referved for the boats, if they made another attempt to land. We then lay four hours without being able to annoy the enemy in the leaft, except from mufkets on the brig, while the fire from the whole fleet was directed againft our buildings. After the third exprefs to New London, fome fixed ammunition arrived. We then turned our cannon on the brig, and fhe foon cut her cable and drifted out.

The whole fleet then weighed, and anchored nearly

out of reach of our fhot, and continued this and the next day to bombard the town.

They fet the buildings on fire in more than twenty places, and we as often put them out. In the three days' bombardment they fent on fhore 60 tons of metal, and, ftrange to fay, wounded only one man, fince dead. We have picked up 15 tons, including fome that was taken up out of the water, and the two anchors that we got.[18] We took up and buried four poor fellows that were hove overboard out of the finking barge.

Since peace, the officers of the *Defpatch* brig have been on fhore here : they acknowledge they had 21 killed, and 50 badly wounded ; and further fay, had we continued our fire any longer, they fhould have ftruck, for they were in a finking condition : for the wind then blew at S. W. directly into the harbour. Before the ammunition arrived, it fhifted round to north, and blew out of the harbour. All the fhot fuitable for the cannon we have referved. We have now more 18 pound fhot than was fent us by government. We have put the two cannon in the arfenal, and houfed all the munitions of war."

EXTRACT FROM THE SPEECH OF GEN. ERASTUS ROOT,
OF NEW YORK,

In the Houfe of Reprefentatives, on the Bill to
provide for the payment of Militia called out by
State authority, and not placed under the command
of the United States.

[After animadverting with great feverity on the affair
at Pettipaug point,[19] and the courfe purfued by
Governor Smith, of Connecticut, for the defence of
New London]—

" There was _one_ achievement, faid Mr. R., which
brightened the annals of Connecticut and fhed luftre
on the American character. He alluded to the _Defence
of Stonington._ A more brilliant affair, faid he, had not
taken place during the late war. It was not rivalled by
the defence of Sandufky, the glorious triumph on the
Niagara, nor the naval victories on Erie and Champ-
lain. And yet that heroic exploit is claimed in favor
of Governor Smith's militia, and is to gild the pill
which we are called upon to fwallow. The detached
militia, faid Mr. R., had nothing to do in that affair.
It was achieved by fourteen democrats, _volunteer_ democrats, who were determined to defend the town or perifh
in its ruins. Commodore Hardy, fearful that that
democratic town would fend torpedoes among his
fquadron, demanded a pledge that no harm fhould be
done to his fhips. No pledge being given, and after

advifing the removal of women and children from the town, the enemy made a vigorous attack, firſt in barges, and afterwards in a brig of war. This heroic little band, with a ſingle gun mounted on a ſmall battery, drove off the brig as they had before driven off the barges. They ſent havoc and death among the enemy,—ſaved the town,—and crowned themſelves with never fading laurels."—*The (Hartford) Times, March* 18, 1817.

THE BATTLE OF STONINGTON, ON THE SEABOARD OF CONNECTICUT.

BY PHILIP FRENEAU.

In an attack upon the town and a ſmall fort of two guns, by the RAMILLIES, *ſeventy-four gun ſhip, commanded by Sir Thomas Hardy; the* PACTOLUS, 38 *gun ſhip;* DESPATCH *brig, and a razee, or bomb ſhip,—Auguſt,* 1814.

Four gallant ſhips from England came
Freighted deep with fire and flame,
And other things we need not name,
          To have a daſh at Stonington.

Now ſafely moor'd, their work begun,
They thought to make the Yankees run,
And have a mighty deal of fun
          In ſtealing ſheep at Stonington.

A deacon then popp'd up his head,
And Parſon Jones's ſermon read,
In which the reverend doctor ſaid
      That they muſt fight for Stonington.

A townſman bade them, next, attend
To ſundry reſolutions penn'd,
By which they promiſed to defend
      With ſword and gun old Stonington.

The ſhips advancing different ways,
The Britons ſoon began to blaze,
And put th' old women in amaze,
      Who feared the loſs of Stonington.

The Yankees to their fort repair'd,
And made as though they little cared
For all that came—though very hard
      The cannon play'd on Stonington.

The *Ramillies* began the attack,
Deſpatch came forward—bold and black—
And none can tell what kept them back
      From ſetting fire to Stonington.

The bombardiers with bomb and ball
Soon made a farmer's barrack fall,
And did a cow-houſe ſadly maul
      That ſtood a mile from Stonington.

They kill'd a goofe, they kill'd a hen,
Three hogs they wounded in a pen—
They dafh'd away,—and pray what then ?
   This was not taking Stonington.

The fhells were thrown, the rockets flew,
But not a fhell, of all they threw,
Though every houfe was full in view,
   Could burn a houfe at Stonington.

To have *their* turn, they thought but fair ;—
The Yankees brought two guns to bear,
And, fir, it would have made you ftare,
   This fmoke of fmokes at Stonington.

They bor'd *Pactolus* through and through,
And kill'd and wounded of her crew
So many, that fhe bade adieu
   T' the gallant boys of Stonington.

The brig *Defpatch* was hull'd and torn—
So crippled, riddled, fo forlorn—
No more fhe caft an eye of fcorn
   On the little fort at Stonington.

The *Ramillies* gave up th' affray,
And, with her comrades fneaked away.
Such was the valor on that day,
   Of Britifh tars, near Stonington.

But fome affert, on certain grounds,
(Befides the damage and the wounds,)
It coft the King ten thoufand pounds
    To have a dafh at Stonington.

[Few of Frenau's earlier and *better* poems were fo popular as this of " The Battle of Stonington," in its day. All Connecticut boys knew it by heart, and it had an eftablifhed place among the ' declamations' of fchool exhibitions. Until within a few years it was to be found in the affortment of every ftreet vender of ballads and patriotic poems,—fometimes in its original form, but more often, with ' emendations and cor-rections.' In the broad-fide from which I firft learned it (bought at a ftall in the neighborhood of Fulton market, fome thirty years ago,) for the twelfth and thirteenth verfes was fubftituted this :—

" They bored the *Defpatch* through and through,
And kill'd and wounded half her crew ;
'Till crippled, riddled, fhe withdrew,—
    And curf'd the boys of Stonington."]

CELEBRATIONS OF THE ANNIVERSARY
OF THE ATTACK.

1815.

Thurſday, Aug. 10th, the firſt anniverſary of the battle, was obſerved as a day of thankſgiving and prayer. The old flag was again hoiſted on the flag-ſtaff at the battery: and a proceſſion, formed at that place, marched to the Congregational meeting-houſe, to liſten to a diſcourſe by the paſtor, Rev. Ira Hart. On its concluſion, the proceſſion returned to the battery, where the exerciſes of the day were cloſed by prayer. " On Friday evening a grand anniverſary ball was given ; the aſſembly being both numerous and brilliant."—*Conn. Gazette, Aug.* 23d.

1818.

Celebration at the Borough, on Monday, Aug. 10th. " The company was very numerous, and the buſineſs of the day went off with great eclat."—*Id. Aug.* 12th, 1818.

1824.

An Oration was delivered at the Congregational meeting-houſe, by Rev. David Auſtin, " characteriſttic of his talents, patriotiſm, and eloquence." The con-courſe of citizens from Stonington and the neighboring towns was unuſually large and reſpectable. An excel-lent dinner was provided by Major Babcock, at the Borough Hotel, to which a large number of citizens and invited guefts did ample juftice. The following were among the volunteer toafts :

By Capt. Edmund Fanning. *The Graffhopper Fort**—may it never be forgotten by thofe whom it defended.

By Samuel Copp, Efq. *American Eighteen-pounders—*as handled in the Graffhopper Fort.

By Gen. J. Ifham. *Auguft* 10*th*, 1814—May no vile calumniator hereafter attempt to tarnifh the hard earned fame of the heroes of that day.

By Gurdon Trumbull, Efq. *John Quincy Adams and Andrew Jackfon*—Their elevation to the firft offices of our government, will demonftrate that fovereignty is yet with the *people*, and guarantee the defence of our national rights, whether affailed by the *pen* or the *fword.*

By Dr. Swift. *Capt. Amos Palmer*—His memory ; his energy and perfeverance.

By W. Storer Jun. *Gen. La Fayette†*—Whom God doth blefs, we will honor.

By Jeffe Dean Efq. *Major Simeon Smith*—Who made cartridges of his ftockings, for our defence, on the day we celebrate.—*New London Gazette, Aug.* 18*th*.

1826.

The inftallation of Benevolent Chapter of Royal Arch Mafons took place at Stonington, on the anniverfary of the attack. The revenue cutters Eagle, from

---

* '' Alluding to a term ufed by the Rev. Orator of the day.''

† Gen. La Fayette's arrival at New York was daily expected. He landed at Caftle Garden, Aug. 16th.

New Haven, the Newport cutter, and the fteamboat
Long-branch (Capt. Mather), from New London,
brought numerous mafonic and other guefts,—military
companies,—and a band of mufic. A proceffion of fome
three hundred brethren and companions was formed,
by order of Doct. Thomas Hubbard, M. E. G. H. P.,
under the direction of Companions Gen. W. Williams,
Samuel F. Denifon, and others, as marfhals. The proceffion marched to the fite of the battery, where a fpa-
cious tent had been erected, with feats for 2500 perfons,—and liftened to a prayer from the Gr. Chaplain,
Rev. Seth B. Paddock, and an Oration by Afa Child,
Efq.; after which the new chapter was dedicated in ample form, and the feveral officers duly inftalled. A
grand dinner clofed the exercifes of the day.—*N. L.
Gazette, Aug.* 16*th.*

1827.

A grand celebration, on the battle ground, where a
a large tent had been erected. Among the guefts were
his Excellency Governor Tomlinfon and his ftaff. The
proceffion formed early in the morning, and marched
through the principal ftreets, efcorted by the Stonington artillery and Norwich rifle companies, to the tent,
—where an addrefs was delivered by Gurdon Trumbull,
Efq.: after which, the proceffion re-formed, and pro-
ceeded to the dinner table (fpread in Mr. Faxon's rope
walk, under the fupervifion of Major Paul Babcock).
Samuel F. Denifon, Efq., prefided at the table, affifted

by Major General Wm. Williams, George Hubbard and B. F. Babcock, Efquires. A long account of the celebration, with the toafts drank at the dinner, &c. —is given in the *New London Gazette*, of Auguft 15th.

N O T E S.

NOTE 1, page 9.

STONINGTON BOROUGH, incorporated by the Legiſlature [of Connecticut,] in 1801, is ſituated on a narrow point of land about half a mile in length, at the eaſtern extremity of Long Iſland ſound. On its eaſtern ſide lies Paucatuck bay, and on its weſt the harbour, terminating in Lambert's Cove. It has four [two] principal ſtreets running north and ſouth, interſected at right angles by nine croſs ſtreets, and contains about one hundred and twenty dwelling houſes and ſtores. It has alſo two houſes for public worſhip, an academy, where the languages are taught, and two common ſchools; two rope-walks, commodious wharves, and ware houſes for ſtorage. . . . In the cenſus of 1810, the *town* contained 3043 inhabitants, and there are now [1819], 335 qualified electors.—*Peaſe & Niles's Gazetteer of Connecticut.*

NOTE 2, page 9.

SIR THOMAS MASTERMAN HARDY, Bart.—afterwards Vice-Admiral, and G. C. B.,—was at this time not far from thirty-five years of age. He entered the British navy, as a midſhipman, at twelve; and was promoted to the rank of commander in 1797, for diſtinguiſhed gallantry in the capture of a French brig, under the walls of Vera Cruz. He commanded the *Mutine* brig, in the battle of the Nile,—became the favorite of Nelſon, and was appointed to the command of his flag-ſhip, ſerving with him, ſucceſſively, in the *Vanguard*, the *Namur*, the *St. George*, (at the battle of Copenhagen), the *Iris* and *Amphitrion*, and the

Victory, on board which Nelſon conquered and fell at Trafalgar. Capt. Hardy was created a baronet, in February, 1806 ; from which period, until 1824, he was almoſt conſtantly on active duty in the Weſt Indies and on American ſtations. He was made a knight commander of the Bath, Jan. 1815, and knight grand cross, in 1831. In October, 1827, he retired from the ſervice ; was appointed a lord of the admiralty in 1830 ; and governor of Greenwich Hoſpital, in 1834, retaining that office until his death, Sept. 20th, 1839.—*Annual Regiſter*, vol. LXXXI, p. 365. *Diſpatches & Letters of Nelſon.*

[Col. Green gave the *ſubſtance* of this note, from memory. A correct copy of it was publiſhed with the official account, in the *Gazette* of Sept. 7th. Commodore Hardy wrote from on board the *Pactolus*,—his own ſhip, the *Ramilies*, then lying at anchor off the weſt end of Fiſher's Iſland.]

NOTE 3, page 10.

CAPT. Amos Palmer, and Dr. Wm. Lord. The former was the ſenior warden of the Borough, and chairman of the committee of citizens who had been entruſted, ſome months previouſly, with the preparations for defence. " He was diſtinguiſhed for his integrity, his republican principles, and his patriotiſm."—*Peaſe & Niles's Gazetteer*, 1819. Capt. Palmer's own account of the attack (in a letter to the Secretary of War,) will be found on pages 33–36. He died at Stonington, March 1, 1816, æt. 69.

NOTE 4, page 10

BRIGADIER-General Thomas H. Cuſhing, who commanded at New London. After the ratification of peace, in 1815, General Cuſhing received the appointment of collector of the port of New London, and retained the office till his death, Oct. 19th, 1822, æt. 67.—*Hiſt. of New London*, p. 649.

An account of the " Bombardment of Stonington" [by the Rev. Frederick Denifon] printed in the *Myftic Pioneer* of July 2d, 1859, contains many interefting particulars, " gathered from the lips of prominent actors in the battle." This account fays, " The firft men, fo far as remembered, that took ftations in the battery, were four, William Lord, Afa Lee, George Fellows, and Amos Denifon. Juft before fix o'clock, fix volunteers from Myftic, Jeremiah Holmes, Jeremiah Haley, Ebenezer Denifon, Ifaac Denifon, and Nathaniel Clift, reached the place, on foot, and ran immediately to help to operate the gun in the battery." . . . . . .

. . . . " The battery being fmall, but few men could work in it, and at this time [later in the morning of the 10th,] it was operated, as nearly as remembered, by Jeremiah Holmes, Simeon Haley, Jeremiah Haley, Ifaac Denifon, Ifaac Miner, George Fellows, and Afa Lee." This lift is not *complete*, but is doubtlefs correct fo far as it relates to the *Myftic* volunteers.

The wound proved mortal. Mr. Denifon died November 1ft, 1814. He was the fourth fon of Ifaac and Eunice [Williams] Denifon, of Myftic, born Dec. 27th, 1795. On the morning of the attack, Frederick,—a youth not yet nineteen years old,—haftened, on foot, to the Borough, to join the little band of volunteers, with whom were already his two elder brothers, Ebenezer and Ifaac, and his brothers-in-law, Capt. Jer. Holmes and Capt. Nath. Clift. He went immediately to the battery, where he helped to work the guns, and during the heat of the action, when the match-rope proved unferviceable, volunteered to go out to procure a new fupply. While on this dangerous errand, he was ftruck by a fhot from the brig, or, as other accounts fay, by a fragment fcaled from a rock by a paffing ball. The wound was not confidered dangerous, and if furgical aid could have been promptly obtained, Mr. Denifon's life might have been fpared.

In May, 1856, the Legiflature of Connecticut made an appropriation for a fuitable monument to his memory, which was erected in Elm Grove Cemetery, at Myftic.—F. D. [*Rev. Fred. Denifon,*] in *Myftic Pioneer*, Aug. 27th, 1859.

Note 7, page 13.

THE colors on the flag ftaff were fhot through nine times. A fence near by was pierced by *fixty-three* balls."—*Myftic Pioneer*. The flag has been carefully preferved, and was in the keeping of Francis Amy, Efq.,—orderly fergeant of Capt. Potter's Company, at the time of the at-tack,—until his death in 1863. Its future prefervation fhould be infured by depofiting it with the Connecticut Hiftory Society.

Note 8, page 13.

JIRAH ISHAM, Efq., commanding the 3d Brigade of the State Mi-litia,—in the 3d Divifion, (William Williams, Efq., Major General.)

. .

Note 9, page 15.

ON Sunday [Aug. 7] a flag came up [to New London] from the frigate *Forth*, Com. Hotham. The object was to obtain permiffion for James Stewart, Efq., formerly conful here, to take off his family. Mr. Stewart was on board. General Cufhing, we underftand, replied that the requeft would be forwarded to Wafhington."—*Conn. Gazette*, Aug. 10th.

Note 10, page 17.

MR. GURDON TRUMBULL was the bearer of this flag, and was accom-panied by Dr. Wm. Lord. The boat was rowed to the *Ramillies* by Noyes Brown and Jabez Holmes. Gen. Ifham's explanation of the firing on Lieut. Claxton, under a flag of truce, had not been received by Com. Hardy when the boat with this letter from the civil authority came along fide. The bearer of the letter was met, at the head of the gang-ladder by a lieutenant, and informed that the Commodore was much incenfed at the infult offered to the flag, and would not receive any communication from the fhore until it fhould be explained. Mr. Trumbull replied that he came as a meffenger from the *civil* and not the *military* authorities, and was not inftructed to offer any explanation : but, as an eye-witnefs of the tranfaction, he would ftate the circumftances, as they occurred. The lieutenant reported thefe to the Commodore, and returned with a meffage that the latter was " perfectly fatiffied ;" that the defenders of the place were fully authorized to prevent the nearer approach of the flag-boat ; and that his officer [Lieut. Claxton] was in the wrong. Mr. Trumbull was then conducted to the cabin, where he found the Commodore, in confultation with all the other commanders of the fquadron, and delivered the letter from the Borough authorities.

Note 11, page 18.

This is not exactly correct. He faid nothing of Mrs. Stewart ; but, after reading the letter, remarked, " I learn from this, Sir, that I am under the neceffity of refuming hoftilities,—which I fhall do, at one o'clock."

Note 12, page 18.

Lieut. John Lathrop, of the Norwich Artillery or " Matrofs Company" (Capt. Charles Thomas). It will be feen, by the narrative of the magiftrates, that Lieut. Lathrop was anticipated in the execution of this fervice, by a party of volunteers.

Note 13, page 19.

Lieut. Samuel L. Hough, of Canterbury, Lieutenant of the L. Infantry Company (Capt. James Afpinwall), detached from the 21ft re-

giment of militia,—in the fervice of the U. States. Lieut. Hough's
wound was not ferious. He is ftill living (June, 1864,)—and in receipt
of a penfion from the U. States.

Note 14, page 24.

THIS account was written by Alex. G. Smith, Efq.

Note 15, page 26.

COL. Wm. Randall, of Stonington, commanding the 30th Regiment of
State Militia.

Note 16, page 31.

Too much praife can hardly be awarded to the volunteer firemen,
who, during the whole of the engagement, continued to patrol the
ftreets, watching the fall of every rocket and fhell, and extinguifhing
fires as foon as lighted. Two of this band may be named without injuftice
to others, as having rendered efficient and conftant fervice,—Capt.
CHARLES H. SMITH and FRANCIS AMY, Efq., both ferjeants in Capt.
Potter's company. Capt. THOMAS SWAN was not lefs active or perfe-
vering. He remained in the Borough, (except for an hour's vifit to his
family, placed in fafety at a farm houfe, a mile diftant,) from the begin-
ning of the attack till the departure of the fhips ; ferving, as neceffity required, with the volunteer firemen, and with the guard ftationed on the
eaft fide of the Point to prevent a landing of the enemy from their boats.

Note 17, page 32.

SEE Capt. Palmer's letter to the Secretary of War, next following.

Note 18, page 36.

THE anchor left by the *Difpatch* brig, at Stonington, when fhe ' cut
and run,' has been got up and brought to New London. It weighs upwards of 20 *cwt.*—*Niles's Weekly Regifter, Sept.* 10, 1814.

" Mr. Chalmers, late mafter of the *Terror*, bomb-veffel, employed in the attack on Stonington, has been captured in a Britifh barge and fent to Providence. He fays 170 bombs were difcharged from that fhip in the attack on Stonington, which were found to weigh 80 lb. each ; the charge of powder for the mortar was 9 lbs. ; adding to this the wadding, that veffel muft have difgorged eight tons weight."—*Ibid.*

" The following appears in a New York paper, in the fhape of an advertifement :

Englifh Manufacture, and Memento of the " Magnanimity" of Commodore Hardy.

Juft received, and offered for fale, about

THREE TONS OF ROUND SHOT,

confifting of 6, 9, 12, 18, 24, and 32 lbs., very handfome, being a *fmall* proportion of thofe which were fired from his Britannic Majefty's fhips, on the unoffending inhabitants of Stonington, in the recent *brilliant* attack on that place.

LIKEWISE, a few *Carcaffes*, in good order, weighing about 200 lbs. each.
Apply to   S. TRUMBULL, 41 *Peck-flip.*
N. B. The purchafer of the above can be fupplied with about *two tons more*, if required.

New York, November 19th, [1814.]"

Niles's Weekly Regifter, Dec. 3d, 1815.

INDUSTRY.—Many of our readers will recollect the anecdote of the thrifty American who afked Commodore *Hardy*, when he would attack *Stonington* again ? fo that he might have his cart ready to carry off the fhot ; and alfo the accounts we have had of the mighty mafs of metal collected there and fold at New York, &c. It feems, however, that the *iron mine* is not yet exhaufted, for certain perfons with a diving machine have raifed no lefs than 11,209 lbs. of fhot, which was thrown overboard from the *Pactolus*, when fhe was in fuch a hurry to get away from the two guns of Stonington!   They have alfo picked up a quantity of copper.— *Niles's Weekly Regifter, June* 3, 1815.

Note 19, page 38.

Capt. Coote, of H. B. M. brig *Borer*, landed two hundred men at Pettipaug, (Saybrook,) in barges and launches, on the 8th of April, 1814, and deftroyed upwards of twenty fail of veffels, without meeting any op-pofition (until after they had re-embarked,) and without the lofs of a man. —*Conn. Gazette, April* 13, 1814.

Letters of Commodore Hardy.

Since the foregoing pages were printed, my friend Professor D. C. Gilman, has brought to my notice the original letters of Commodore Hardy, to the inhabitants of Stonington and to General Isham, which are now in the Library of Yale College. The first (of August 9th) was copied with sufficient accuracy in the account published by the magistrates, warden and burgesses (page 25), I reprint it here, but with a fac simile of the signature.

> *His Britannic Majesty's Ship,*
> PACTOLUS, *9th August,* 1814.
> $\frac{1}{2}$ *past* 5 *o'clock, P. M.*

Not wishing to destroy the unoffending Inhabitants residing in the Town of Stonington, one hour is granted them from the receipt of this to remove out of the town.

[signature: T. M. Hardy Captain of H.M. Ship Ramillies]

To the Inhabitants of the Town of Stonington.

The fecond, is in reply to the letter from the magiftrates which was fent on board the *Ramillies*, by Col. Isaac Williams and Dr. William Lord, on Wednefday, the 10th. As "official etiquette" did not permit Col. Green to obtain "an exact copy," he could only print its fubftance "as far as memory ferved" (fee page 14). The magiftrates allude to it, in their publifhed account (p. 30), as "the fingular communication received from Commodore Hardy, which preceded the fire on Thurf-day." It is evident that the Britifh commander was ftrangely in error as to the affurances and engagements which he profeffed to have received, or that the gentlemen entrufted with the delivery of the letter from the magiftrates muft, in their conference with the Commodore, have exceeded their inftructions.

> *Ramillies, off Stonington,*
> *10th August,* 1814.

GENT[N]

I have received your letter and reprefentation of the State of your Town, and as you have declared that Torpedoes, never have been harbored by the Inhabit-ants or ever will be, as far as lies in their power to prevent — and as you have engaged that Mrs. Stewart the wife of the Britifh vice conful late refident at New London, with her family, fhall be permitted to embark on board this Ship to-morrow morning, I am induced to wave the attempt of the total deftruction of your Town, which I feel confident can be effected by the Squadron under my Orders.

> I am
> Gent[n]
> Your moft obedient fervant,
> T. M. HARDY, Captain.

To Doctor LAW [*Lord*] *and Colonel* WILLIAMS,
> *Stonington.*

In reprinting the refponfe of the civil authorities of Stonington, to the foregoing letter, on page 17, *ante*, an error in the date fhould have been corrected.   It was written and defpatched on the *eleventh* of Auguft.

The following note acknowledges the explanation fent by General Ifham, of the circumftances under which a flag of truce from the *Ramillies*, was fired upon by a fentinel at the Battery, on the morning of the 11th (fee pages 16, 17, and note 10).

Ramillies, off Stonington,
11th Auguft, 1814.

Sir,

I have the honor to acknowledge the receipt of your letter, apologizing for the Flag of Truce I fent on fhore this morning, having been fired at ; and I beg to affure you that under the Circumftances you have ftated, the apology is perfectly fatisfactory.

I have the honor to be, Sir,
Your moft obedient
humble Servant,
T. M. Hardy, Captain.

To Brigadier Isham — *Commanding at Stonington.*